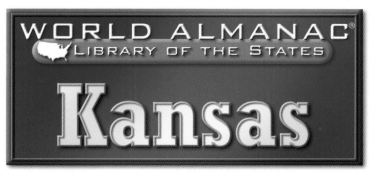

# THE SUNFLOWER STATE

*by W. Scott Ingram*

Curriculum Consultant: Jean Craven,
Director of Instructional Support,
Albuquerque, NM, Public Schools

**WORLD ALMANAC® LIBRARY**

**Please visit our web site at: www.worldalmanaclibrary.com**
**For a free color catalog describing World Almanac® Library's**
**list of high-quality books and multimedia programs, call**
**1-800-848-2928 (USA) or 1-800-387-3178 (Canada).**
**World Almanac® Library's fax: (414) 332-3567.**

**Library of Congress Cataloging-in-Publication Data**

Ingram, Scott (William Scott).
    Kansas, the Sunflower State / by W. Scott Ingram.
      p. cm. — (World Almanac Library of the states)
    Includes bibliographical references and index.
    Summary: Presents the history, geography, people, politics and government,
economy, social life and customs, state events and attractions, and notable people
of Kansas, which is named for the Kaw (Kansa) Indians.
    ISBN 0-8368-5134-X (lib. bdg.)
    ISBN 0-8368-5304-0 (softcover)
    1. Kansas—Juvenile literature. [1. Kansas.] I. Title. II. Series.
F681.3.I53   2002
978.1—dc21                         2002016885

This edition first published in 2002 by
**World Almanac® Library**
330 West Olive Street, Suite 100
Milwaukee, WI 53212 USA

This edition © 2002 by World Almanac® Library.

Design and Editorial: Bill SMITH STUDIO Inc.
Editor: Kristen Behrens
Assistant Editor: Megan Elias
Art Director: Jay Jaffe
Photo Research: Sean Livingstone
World Almanac® Library Project Editor: Patricia Lantier
World Almanac® Library Editors: Monica Rausch, Jim Mezzanotte
World Almanac® Library Production: Scott M. Krall, Tammy Gruenewald,
  Katherine A. Goedheer

Photo credits: p. 4 © Corel; p. 6 (bottom) © Corel; (top) © PhotoDisc; p. 7 (top) © PhotoDisc;
(bottom) © ArtToday; p. 9 © Corel; p. 10 © Tom Bean/CORBIS; p. 11 © ArtToday; p. 12 © Library
of Congress; p. 13 all Dover Publications; p. 14 © Margaret Bourke-White/TimePix; p. 15 (top)
© Carl Iwasaki/TimePix; (bottom) © Vince Streano/CORBIS; p. 17 © Bettmann/CORBIS; p. 18
Topeka CVB; p. 19 Topeka CVB; p. 20 (left to right) © Corbis; © Corel; © Corel; p. 21 (left to right)
© Corbis; © PAINET INC.; © PhotoSpin; p. 23 © Corel; p. 24 © PhotoDisc; p. 26 (top)
© PhotoDisc; (bottom) © Corel; p. 27 © PhotoDisc; p. 29 Topeka CVB; p. 30 Topeka CVB; p. 31
© Library of Congress; p. 32 Topeka CVB; p. 33 Topeka CVB; p. 34 courtesy of Rolling Hills
Refuge; p. 35 © David G. Houser/CORBIS; p. 36 © PhotoDisc; p. 37 (top) © George Silk/TimePix;
(bottom) Dover Publications; p. 38 (left) Dover; (right) © Bettmann/CORBIS; p. 39 © Johnson
Library of Congress; p. 41 (all) © PhotoDisc; pp. 42–43 © Library of Congress; p. 44 (all)
© PhotoDisc; p. 45 (top) © Corel; (bottom) © Painet Inc.

Printed in the United States of America

1 2 3 4 5 6 7 8 9 06 05 04 03 02

# Kansas

# Colorful Kansas

The Sunflower State is located almost exactly in the middle of the United States in an area known as the Midwest. In the 1800s, Kansas was not the Midwest — it was the Wild West. Cowboys drove cattle across Kansas for fifty important years in U.S. history, during the last half of the nineteenth century. Railroads crisscrossed the state like steel spider webs. Dusty towns such as Wichita, Dodge City, and Abilene served as railroad yards to ship cattle east to meat packers. These towns became some of the most legendary settings of the Old West.

In the late 1800s, Kansas was home to many of the men and women who helped create the legends of the Wild West. Lawmen such as Wyatt Earp, cowboys like Nat Love, and a host of outlaws are part of Kansas history.

Kansas, however, is more than cowboys and cattle. Long before Europeans crossed into Kansas, Native Americans roamed the region following their main food, bison. In fact, the name *Kansas* is taken from a tribe called the Kansa or Kaw, who lived in the northeastern part of the state. The Kaw, as well as the Comanche, Osage, and Pawnee, lived off the enormous herds of bison that flowed like waves across a green ocean of prairie grass.

Kansas is also more than a location on a map. From prehistoric seas to oceans of wheat, the state has a fascinating story to tell. It is the story of prairie trails that carried pioneers west. It is the story of people such as Amelia Earhart, the first woman to fly across the Atlantic Ocean, and Dwight D. Eisenhower, the nation's heroic thirty-fourth president. It is the story of natural events, such as tornadoes, and human events, such as the battles of "Bleeding Kansas" that helped set the stage for the Civil War. Kansas may be a plains state — but there is nothing plain about it.

▶ Map of Kansas showing the interstate highway system, as well as major cities and waterways.

▼ A field of Kansas sunflowers.

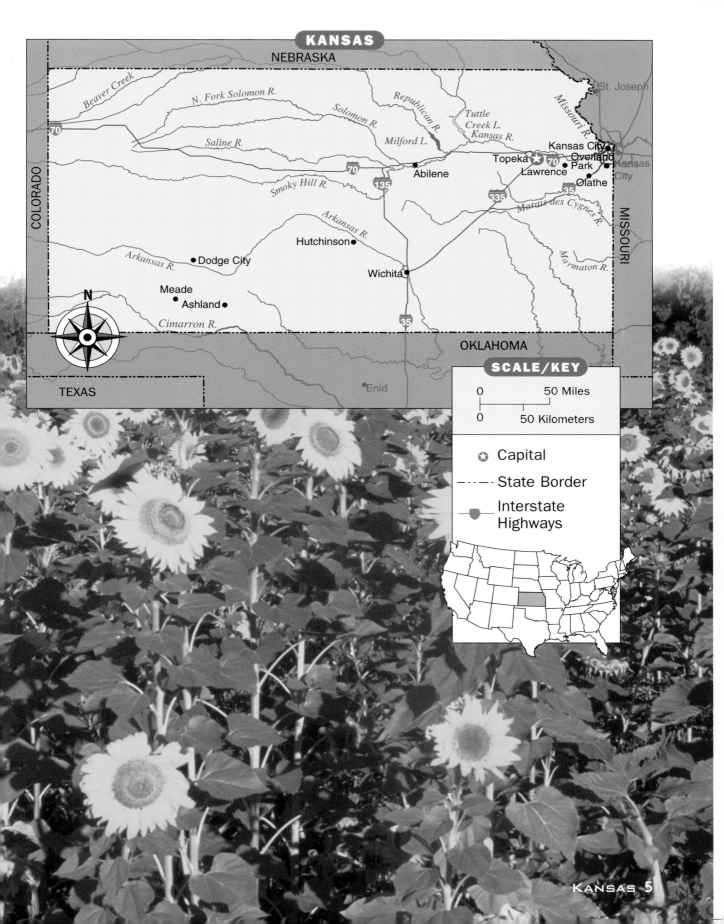

KANSAS

NEBRASKA

COLORADO

Beaver Creek

N. Fork Solomon R.

Republican R.

Solomon R.

Saline R.

Milford L.

Tuttle Creek L.

Kansas R.

Missouri R.

St. Joseph

Topeka ★

Abilene

Kansas City

Overland Park

Lawrence

Olathe

Kansas City

Smoky Hill R.

Arkansas R.

Hutchinson

Marais des Cygnes R.

MISSOURI

Arkansas R.

Dodge City

Wichita

Marmaton R.

Meade

Ashland

Cimarron R.

OKLAHOMA

TEXAS

Enid

# Fast Facts

## KANSAS (KS), The Sunflower State

**KANSAS**

### Entered Union
January 29, 1861 (34th State)

| Capital | Population |
|---|---|
| Topeka | 122,377 |

### Total Population (2000)
2,688,418 (32nd most populous state) — *Between 1990 and 2000, the population of Kansas increased by 8.5 percent.*

| Largest Cities | Population |
|---|---|
| Wichita | 344,284 |
| Overland Park | 149,080 |
| Kansas City | 146,866 |
| Topeka | 122,377 |
| Olathe | 92,962 |

### Land Area
81,815 square miles (211,901 square kilometers) (13th largest state)

### State Motto
Ad Astra per Aspera — *Latin for "To the Stars Through Difficulty."*

### State Song
"Home on the Range," *by Dr. Brewster Higley and Daniel Kelley.*

### State Animal
American buffalo, or bison — *The Kansas state song begins with the words "Oh give me a home where the buffalo roam."*

### State Bird
Western meadowlark — *The state bird was chosen by Kansas schoolchildren.*

### State Insect
Honeybee

### State Tree
Cottonwood

### State Flower
Native sunflower — *Kansans like sunflowers so much that they put one on their state banner. State banners are flown on ceremonial occasions.*

### State Reptile
Ornate box turtle — *Tina the box turtle traveled the state in 1986 as part of the successful campaign to get this brown and yellow animal declared the official state reptile.*

### State Amphibian
Barred tiger salamander — *This striped Kansas creature is at home everywhere, from the prairies in the eastern part of the state to the dry plains in the west.*

## PLACES TO VISIT

**Stan Herd's Crop Art,** *Lawrence*
Internationally recognized artist Stan Herd uses his native state to create gigantic works of art — he mows crop fields into portraits and still lifes.

**Smoky Hills Region,** *west of Flint Hills*
This region is home to a wide variety of interesting rock formations, including Castle Rock, Monument Rocks, and the Mushroom Rocks of Ellsworth.

**Garden of Eden,** *Lucas*
In 1905, Samuel P. Dinsmoor of Lucas began to build his Garden of Eden out of cement. Everything in the garden, including flowers, strawberries, and a fish pool, is made out of cement.

**For other places and events, see p. 44.**

## BIGGEST, BEST, AND MOST

- The Rock Island Railway Bridge, south of Ashland, is the longest wood-and-post bridge ever built. It is 1,200 feet (366 meters) long and stands 100 feet (30 m) above the Cimarron River.

- Smith County is the geographical center of the "lower" forty-eight states.

## STATE FIRSTS

- **1877** Nicodemus, the oldest existing town established entirely by African Americans, was founded. It was named after a legendary African prince who was supposedly the first slave to buy his freedom.

- **1887** Susanna Madora Salter was elected mayor of Argonia, making her the first woman ever elected mayor of a U.S. city. Salter's name had been placed on the ballot without her knowledge, and she did not find out until she went to vote.

- **1970** Elizabeth P. Hoisington of Newton became the first female U.S. Army brigadier general.

## Space Cowboys

In 1897, Alexander Hamilton of Yates Center reported that strange creatures in a flying saucer had lassoed one of his calves and tried to pull it onto their ship. Hamilton beat off the rustlers, and the story was published in the local newspaper. Other newspapers then picked up Hamilton's story, and it became one of the classic tales of alien encounters. What no one outside of Yates Center knew, however, was that Hamilton and his friends were members of a Liars Club. Members of the club tried to trick each other with tall tales. It wasn't until 1977 that the hoax was uncovered.

## Kansas Luck

In 1911, a Kansas farmer approached John McGraw, the manager of the New York Giants baseball team. The farmer, Charles Faust, told McGraw that a fortune-teller had told him if he pitched for the Giants they would win the pennant. Faust was not much of a pitcher, but because McGraw was superstitious he let Faust wear a uniform, warm up with the team, and sit on the bench. For the next three years, with Charles "Victory" Faust on the bench (and on two occasions actually pitching), the fortune-teller's promise came true and the Giants won the National League pennant.

# From Ocean Floor to Fertile Plains

> The story of the dangers braved, the privations endured, the sacrifices made, the sufferings borne, which, out of great tribulation have wrought such happy issues for the people of later times, constitutes the history of Kansas.
>
> — *William G. Cutler*, History of the State of Kansas, *1883*

Eighty-five million years ago, Kansas was at the bottom of an ocean. Scientists today have named this ocean the Western Interior Sea. Fossilized bones from giant swimming and flying reptiles have been discovered in the western part of the state. Wagon trains traveling across western Kansas in the early 1800s passed Castle Rock and Monument Rocks. Erosion carved these famous landmarks from chalk deposited by ancient seas. Although they called their wagons "prairie schooners," after a type of boat, pioneers never imagined that they were really crossing an ancient ocean floor.

It took millions of years, but the oceans dried up, revealing land that we know today as Kansas. About two hundred thousand years ago, a shaggy, grazing animal — the American buffalo, or bison — made its way to North America's Great Plains. The first people to live in Kansas may have followed the bison across North America, hunting the large animal for food, clothing, shelter, and tools.

## Native People and Explorers

Native Americans lived off the bison for centuries, even though hunting the large beasts on foot was dangerous and difficult. Hunting bison became less risky in 1541, when Spanish explorer Francisco Vásquez de Coronado entered present-day Kansas searching for gold. He and his men did not find gold, but they left some horses behind. The horse became one of the Plains tribes' most valuable possessions. The Comanche, the Dakota (also known as the Sioux), and the Ute became skilled horseback riders who hunted bison with bows and arrows.

| Native Americans of Kansas |
| --- |
| Arapahoe |
| Cheyenne |
| Comanche |
| Dakota (Sioux) |
| Kaw (Kansa) |
| Kiowa |
| Omaha |
| Osage |
| Pawnee |
| Peoria |
| Potawatomi |
| Shawnee |
| Ute |
| Wichita |
| Wyandot |

### DID YOU KNOW?

The name *Kansas* comes from the name for the Kaw, or Kansa. The word means "the land of the Wind People" or "the land of the People of the South Wind."

Between 1550 and 1750, more and more Europeans arrived in North America. In time, they moved west, pushing Native Americans such as the Kaw, the Osage, and the Omaha farther west. Around 1750, the tribes from what today are Ohio and Kentucky moved west down the Ohio River to the Missouri River near the current site of St. Louis. From there the tribes split, and the Kaw tribe settled in the lands around the Kansas River Valley. By the end of the 1700s, the Kaw controlled most of northern and eastern Kansas.

## The Movement West

In 1803, President Thomas Jefferson signed an agreement with France to purchase the land west of the Mississippi for $15 million. The Louisiana Purchase opened up most of the Great Plains to explorers and traders.

In the spring of 1804, President Jefferson sent a group of explorers led by Captain Meriwether Lewis and Lieutenant William Clark on an "expedition of discovery." Lewis and Clark passed briefly through Kansas on their way to the Pacific Ocean, charting a route that opened the West.

Other explorers soon followed. In 1822, William Becknell, a trader from Missouri, followed a 750-mile (1,207-km) trail from Missouri to the Arkansas River (today the site of Dodge City), then south to the Cimarron River. Much of the trail passed through Kansas. This became the Santa Fe Trail — the first trail large and flat enough to accommodate wagons.

The Santa Fe Trail soon brought an end to a way of life for the Kaw and other Native Americans who had built villages and farms along the Kansas River. In 1825, the Osage and Kaw tribes signed a treaty with the U.S. government allowing the trail to pass through their lands.

▲ Albert Bierstadt's painting *The Wolf River* (1859) depicts the arrival of traders at a Native American camp.

In 1830, President Andrew Jackson signed the Indian Removal Act. Under this law, the U.S. government could force Native Americans off their lands east of the Mississippi River. Most Native Americans were moved to northeastern Kansas onto land that was controlled by the Kaw and the Osage. Although this area was supposed to be Native American territory, control was gradually lost to the U.S. government and the surge of white settlers.

Besides the Santa Fe Trail, pioneers took another path through Kansas — the Oregon Trail. Between 1840 and 1860, more than 300,000 people crossed Kansas on their way to Oregon and California. The United States set up military posts to offer help and protection to the large number of people crossing the open plains. Posts such as Fort Scott and Fort Leavenworth became towns when Kansas was settled.

## Settlers and Slavery

Those who settled in Kansas in the first half of the 1800s faced a difficult issue — slavery. The nation had long been divided between the belief that slavery was wrong and the federal government should abolish it, and the belief that slave ownership was a right.

As the lands west of the Mississippi were occupied by settlers from both the North and the South, the debate over

### Native American Relocation

Sources vary widely about how many Native Americans were moved west. As many as one hundred thousand may have been forced to relocate. Some of the dozens of tribes forced from their lands included the Shawnee, Wyandot, Miami, Peoria, and Potawatomi — tribes whose names are given to places in Kansas today.

▼ Santa Fe Trail markers still stand in the Cimarron National Grassland in Elkhart.

allowing slavery in newly settled territories grew. Lawmakers in Washington, D.C., settled the first disagreements with the 1820 Missouri Compromise. It admitted Missouri as a slave state and Maine as a free state, which kept the voting balance even in the U.S. Senate. Both sides agreed to prohibit slavery in any territories north of Missouri's southern border.

Throughout the next thirty years, however, disagreement over slavery grew increasingly bitter across the United States. That bitterness became violent in Kansas in the mid-1850s. Until 1854, the only non-Natives in Kansas were living at military posts, trading posts, or religious missions. Then, Congress passed the Kansas–Nebraska Act of 1854, which created two territories — Kansas and Nebraska — from one large land area. Nebraska, north of Missouri, was declared a free state. Southern lawmakers, however, wanted slavery to be legal in Kansas, even though Kansas was north of Missouri's southern border. Lawmakers in Congress decided to leave the decision up to the citizens of Kansas. They said the slavery issue would be decided by "popular sovereignty" — a majority vote by the territory's white residents. Thus the Kansas–Nebraska Act superseded the Missouri Compromise. Suddenly there was a race between pro- and antislavery settlers for control of Kansas.

Antislavery northerners moved to Kansas, hoping to make it a free state. Settlers from the nearby slave state of Missouri also moved in, hoping to accomplish the opposite. By 1855, antislavery settlers called "Free Soilers" had set up a territorial government in Lawrence. Pro-slavery settlers voted to allow slavery in the southeastern part of Kansas and established another territorial government there.

## "Bleeding Kansas"

In 1856, pro-slavery forces began a campaign of violence in an attempt to make the Kansas Territory a slave state. They raided the antislavery town of Lawrence, destroying

▲ This etching depicts one of many violent episodes that occurred in the Kansas Territory following the passage of the Kansas-Nebraska Act. The territory was virtually at war as pro-slavery and antislavery forces fought to control how Kansas entered the Union — as a slave state or a free state.

a number of buildings. Free Soilers fought back, initially led by militant abolitionist John Brown. In retaliation for the attack on Lawrence, Brown led a group of men, including four of his sons, on a raid against a pro-slavery settlement in Pottawatomie Creek. Brown and his group killed five men. Brown then successfully held off a retaliatory raid on his own settlement of Osawatomie.

The fighting continued, and the territory became known as "Bleeding Kansas." By 1858, more than fifty skirmishes and raids had taken place until the final massacre on the Marais des Cygnes River. Free Staters took control of the state a year later and banned slavery. Kansas was admitted to the Union as a free state in 1861, five weeks before Abraham Lincoln took office as the sixteenth president. Three months later, the Civil War began — a war in which the first shots, many believed, had already been fired in Kansas.

The Civil War did not stop people from coming to Kansas. A new wave of settlers came to the state after Congress passed the Homestead Act of 1862, which offered 160 acres (65 hectares) to anyone who would build on the land and live there for five years. Settlers who paid $1.25 per acre ($3.00 per ha) and lived on their parcel for six months could also claim ownership. Native Americans, who were not considered citizens, could not claim any land. In fact, the Homestead Act forced them farther west.

## Postwar Kansas

In the years following the Civil War, the U.S. government gave away thousands of acres, not only to settlers but also to the increasingly powerful railroad companies. With the East and West Coasts connected by the transcontinental railroad in 1869, land in Kansas became an important prize for competing railway companies. The state's relatively flat land was perfect for laying track. Between 1869 and 1873, five different railroad companies laid rails across Kansas.

The flood of settlers and railroad companies into the state brought enormous changes to the Native Americans. More land for the trains and towns meant less land for the

### On the Move

**A**fter the Civil War, slavery was outlawed but racial violence continued in the South. More than forty thousand African Americans, fearing for their lives, moved north to Kansas. They migrated in such large numbers that they became known as the Exodusters after "Exodus," a book in the Bible in which all of the Jews fled from Egypt, where they had been enslaved. Exodusters established the Kansas town of Nicodemus, which was the first town west of the Mississippi to be founded by African Americans. Nicodemus, which is now a National Historic Site, was one of about a dozen African-American towns settled by the Exodusters.

Native Americans and the bison. Hunters were brought in to kill as many bison as possible to keep them from wandering onto railroad tracks. "Buffalo Bill" Cody — later a famous showman — received his nickname for his hunting exploits. He killed more than 2,800 bison in a seventeen-month period. Cody sold some of the carcasses to a railroad company to feed its work crews, while others he simply left to rot.

By 1889, about eight hundred bison were left alive in the United States. With their food supply almost gone, Native Americans were forced onto smaller reservations on undesirable land. By the late 1800s, most of the Native American tribes of Kansas had been relocated to Indian Territory, in present-day Oklahoma.

As the bison disappeared, other animals became important to the state. Longhorn cattle raised in Texas began to make the journey north to Kansas, where they would be shipped east to supply beef for the growing population there. From 1867 to 1872, more than three million head of cattle were driven up the Chisholm Trail from Texas to Abilene, Kansas. Cow towns were built up, following the extension of the railroads west. By 1870, towns such as Dodge City, Abilene, Caldwell, Newton, and Wichita were all trail heads for cowboys and the herds they drove to market. Between 1875 and 1886, more than five million cattle arrived in Kansas from Texas.

In 1874, a new group arrived in Kansas. They were members of a religious group called the Mennonites, and they brought with them Turkey Red winter wheat, a grain crop that was perfectly suited for the dry plains of Kansas. At the time, corn grown in eastern Kansas was

# The Wild West

**A**t the end of the cattle trails, trouble brewed. Once the cowboys were paid for their work, many spent their money wildly, and, after many lonely weeks on the dusty trail, they often became rowdy. Fights were a daily occurrence. Abilene and Dodge City became known as the roughest towns in the West. There were so many deaths from the gunfights in Dodge City that the local cemetery became known as Boot Hill after the great number of its residents who had died "with their boots on." Two of the most famous lawmen of western lore, Bat Masterson (*above, left*) and Wyatt Earp (*above, right*), began their careers in Kansas. These law officers, often as violent as the men they arrested, eventually brought law and order to Dodge City, Abilene, and other Kansas cow towns.

the state's main crop. Turkey Red wheat could be harvested in spring, so it did not get ruined by summer heat and insects. The popularity of the crop grew, and Kansans set up flour mills to process the wheat. The state became known as the "Breadbasket of the United States" and continues to be the world's leading wheat producer.

## The Twentieth Century

By the end of the nineteenth century, Kansas was a major supplier of the country's beef and wheat. The early 1900s saw the development and growth of mining, oil production, meatpacking, and automobile manufacturing. The flat plains and wide-open skies of Kansas made the state a perfect location for an industry built on a new way of travel — flying. Some of the most famous aircraft manufacturers — Cessna, Beech, Lear, Steer, and others — built their first plants in Kansas. One person to be swept up in the early excitement of airplanes was Amelia Earhart, a pioneer aviator from Atchison.

Kansas, along with the rest of the United States and much of the world, entered a period called the Great Depression in the 1930s. It was a time when banks closed, people lost their jobs, and a drought brought disaster to millions of farmers throughout the Midwest. Kansas was hit hard by the Depression because of its large number of farms. Sod, the tough, grassy surface of the plains, had held Kansas's rich soil in place for millions of years, but farmers had plowed up this sod to plant crops. After several years of severe drought, the soil dried up and blew away. So much soil blew off the plains in the dust storms of 1935 to 1938 that Kansas and other affected states became known as "The Dust Bowl." Thousands left the state to seek better lives elsewhere.

After 1938, rain began to fall in normal amounts again, and federal projects helped farmers irrigate and protect the soil. The economy of Kansas did not fully recover until the United States entered World War II in 1941. Kansas wheat

### DID YOU KNOW?

In 1920, a Laird Swallow, the first commercially produced U.S. airplane, made its first flight over Wichita, earning the city its nickname "Air Capital of the World."

and beef were used to feed soldiers and civilians, and Kansas aircraft companies built warplanes, from bombers to gliders. Twenty-five thousand new jobs were created in the aircraft manufacturing plants in Kansas. During the war, 50 to 60 percent of the jobs in these plants were held by women. Manufacturing continued to grow throughout the 1950s and 1960s as aerospace companies began to build rockets for the initial space program. In 1952, war hero General Dwight D. Eisenhower of Abilene was elected U.S. president.

In the 1950s, Topeka, Kansas, became the center of a national crisis over racial segregation. In Topeka, as in many other places in the nation, African-American and white children attended separate schools. Schools for both groups of children were supposed to be of equal quality, but African-American schools were not provided with good buildings or books and had fewer teachers per student. Oliver Brown, the father of a third-grader, took the nearest white school to court in 1951, demanding that it allow his daughter to attend. When the Supreme Court heard the case, *Brown v. The Board of Education of Topeka, Kansas,* it found in favor of the Browns and in 1954 declared segregation in education unconstitutional.

By the end of the twentieth century, Kansas had grown from being mainly an agricultural state to a state with both large industrial and agricultural businesses. The death of the last full-blooded Kaw, eighty-two-year-old William Mehojah, on April 23, 2000, is a moving reminder of the changes Kansas has experienced, from its earliest days to the beginning of a new millennium.

▲ Oliver Brown (*right*) fought for the civil right of his daughter Linda (*left*) to attend a white school near their home. Brown's court suit began the desegregation of U.S. schools.

▼ Since the late nineteenth century, cattle-raising and its related industries have provided significant sources of income in Kansas.

# People of the Sunflower State

> I'm as corny as Kansas in August,
> I'm as normal as blueberry pie.
>
> — Oscar Hammerstein, "A Wonderful Guy,"
> from the 1949 musical South Pacific

Until the early 1850s, there were few settlers in Kansas. After the Civil War, railroads and the availability of cheap land attracted a wave of settlers from the eastern United States as well as western and central Europe that continued through the end of the nineteenth century. Immigration slowed in the twentieth century. During World War II, there was an influx of servicemen and aircraft workers, many of whom settled in the state. Most modern-day Kansans are of European descent.

## Kansas Today

Although Kansas is the thirteenth-largest state in terms of land area, it ranks only thirty-second in total population. The combination of a large land area and a relatively small population results in an interesting statistic — there are only 32.9 people per square mile (13 per sq km) in the

### Age Distribution in Kansas
(2000 Census)

| | |
|---|---|
| 0–4 | 188,708 |
| 5–19 | 609,710 |
| 20–24 | 190,167 |
| 25–44 | 769,204 |
| 45–64 | 574,400 |
| 65 & over | 356,229 |

## Across One Hundred Years

### Kansas's three largest foreign-born groups for 1890 and 1990

Legend: ■ 1890  ■ 1990

| Germany 46,423 | England 18,080 | Sweden 17,096 | Mexico 14,919 | Germany 5,003 | Vietnam 4,616 |

**Total state population: 1,427,096**
**Total foreign-born: 147,838 (10%)**

**Total state population: 2,477,574**
**Total foreign-born: 62,840 (3%)**

### Patterns of Immigration

The total number of people who immigrated to Kansas in 1998 was 3,184. Of that number, the largest immigrant groups were from Mexico (42.6%), Vietnam (8.8%), and India (5.8%).

### Orphans Away

In the 1870s, charity workers in New York City estimated that there were about thirty thousand children without parents living on the streets. The New York Children's Aid Society workers decided that these children would be better off on the western frontier, where they could live with farming families and work in fresh air. They were able to interest western farm families in the plan because a farm always needs extra workers. The charity workers also allowed families to return orphans they didn't want. Between 1877 and 1930, more than 150,000 children traveled west on special "orphan trains" to start new lives.

state. In other words, the population density of Kansas is much lower than the nation as a whole, which has almost 80 people per square mile (30 per sq km). Like the rest of the U.S. population, the number of older people in Kansas has grown. The median age in the state is 35.8 years, about the same as the rest of the nation. The median income of Kansans is $37,705 per year, about $500 below the national average, but the cost of living is also significantly less.

The population of Kansas is predominantly white. At more than 86 percent, the percentage of white Kansans is 10 percent higher than the overall national percentage.

Although the average number of Kansans per square mile is low, more than two-thirds of all state residents live in cities. The once dusty cow towns of Kansas are now

## Heritage and Background, Kansas — Year 2000

▶ Here's a look at the racial backgrounds of Kansans today. Kansas ranks thirty-first among all U.S. states with regard to African Americans as a percentage of the population.

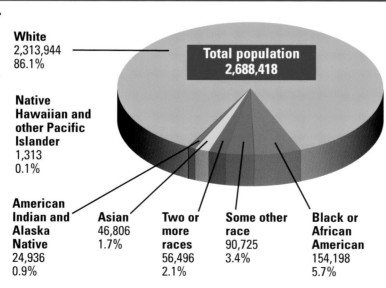

Total population 2,688,418

White 2,313,944 86.1%

Native Hawaiian and other Pacific Islander 1,313 0.1%

American Indian and Alaska Native 24,936 0.9%

Asian 46,806 1.7%

Two or more races 56,496 2.1%

Some other race 90,725 3.4%

Black or African American 154,198 5.7%

**Note:** 7.0% (188,252) of the population identify themselves as **Hispanic** or **Latino,** a cultural designation that crosses racial lines. Hispanics and Latinos are counted in this category as well as the racial category of their choice.

paved with concrete. Cars, not cows, travel down the streets of Abilene and Dodge City, and people live in houses of wood and brick instead of sod. Wichita, Kansas City, and Topeka are three of the largest cities in the state, and all three are in the eastern half of Kansas. Western Kansas is mostly rural, with farmers, ranchers, and modern-day cowboys, but getting from town to town is easy. The state turnpike, an interstate route, was completed in 1956. Kansas has over 133,000 miles (214,000 km) of state, city, and county roads.

## Education

The first schools in Kansas were established by Christian missionaries during the 1830s to educate Native American children. Some non-Native children attended these schools before public school education was available. In 1855, Kansas lawmakers took steps to provide free education

| Educational Levels of Kansas Workers (age 25 and over) | |
| --- | --- |
| Less than 9th grade | 120,951 |
| 9th to 12th grade, no diploma | 172,321 |
| High school graduate, including equivalency | 514,177 |
| Some college, no degree or associate degree | 428,110 |
| Bachelor's degree | 221,016 |
| Graduate or professional degree | 109,361 |

▼ The skyline of Topeka, capital of Kansas and its fourth-largest city.

for white children in the Kansas Territory. In 1859, the territorial legislature expanded education to include all children in Kansas. Today, Kansas law requires all children between the ages of seven and sixteen to attend school. An elected state board of education controls the school system. The board appoints a commissioner to oversee elementary and secondary education. Local boards and superintendents direct schools at the district level. In 1963, many small, local school districts in Kansas were combined to make better use of school facilities. The state's educational system now comprises more than five hundred Unified School Districts (USDs).

Kansas is also home to more than twenty-five colleges and universities, including two public university systems — the University of Kansas and Kansas State University. As the urban centers in Kansas are relatively small, cultural life tends to center in university towns. Kansas has about twenty community colleges, as well as fifteen post-high school vocational schools to provide job training.

▲ Located in Manhattan, Kansas, Kansas State University is home base for fans of the KSU Wildcats.

## Religion

The first settlers in Kansas were Protestants. Today, Protestant churches still have the largest membership in the state, with 77 percent of the population attending the many denominations of Protestant Christian faiths. Sixteen percent of Kansans are Roman Catholic. Among other faiths, 0.9 percent of Kansans practice Native American religions, 0.6 percent practice Judaism, 0.3 percent practice Buddhism, 0.1 percent practice Hinduism, and 0.1 percent practice Islam.

# Sunflower Country

> . . . The swelling surface of the prairie . . . lofty table lands overlooking great rivers . . . bluffs and hills lifting their bold graceful outlines against the sky; everywhere delight the eye and redeem the landscape from monotony.
>
> — *March 1857 broadside "Information for Emigrants to Kansas," printed by the National Kansas Committee*

**M**ost people outside of Kansas think of the Sunflower State as the flat, dry, dusty, tornado-filled place seen in the movie *The Wizard of Oz*. That Kansas, however, was actually a Hollywood studio. The real Kansas is a land of amazing variety — hilly in the southeast and flat in parts of the west. It features oceanlike grasslands; shallow, winding rivers; and endless fields of grain.

Like Oklahoma, Wyoming, Nebraska, and Colorado, Kansas is one of the states on the Great Plains. Most of this land was formed beneath an enormous prehistoric ocean. For that reason, Kansas has some of the richest fossil deposits in the world, especially in the western regions.

Although many people think of Kansas as flat, the state is on an incline. Its highest point is 4,039 feet (1,231 m) above sea level at Mount Sunflower in the northwest near the Colorado line. From there, it slopes downward to the lowest point in the southeast at 679 feet (207 m) above sea level, where the Verdigris River flows into Oklahoma.

**Highest Point**
**Mt. Sunflower**
4,039 feet (1,231 m)
above sea level

▼ *From left to right:* a tornado touches down; a peregrine falcon at rest; a field of sunflowers; the Prairie Park Nature Center, which contains more than 180 species of native plants; a rattlesnake; Pedestal Rock.

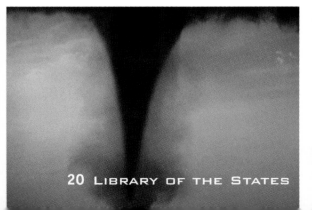

## A Varied Landscape

Kansas is not just a plains state. The southeast corner of the state, the Ozark Plateau and Cherokee Lowlands, is hilly and covered in trees. North of this region is the Osage Cuesta, a region of special hills that have steep slopes on the northern sides and gentle slopes on the southern sides.

The first settlers in Kansas passed by the Flint Hills in the east-central part of the state searching for good farmland. Few people settled there because the land was not suitable for farming. Today, this area is home to the largest unplowed tract of prairie in the United States. The tract is covered with hundreds of native prairie grasses.

The western part of the state is known as post-rock country because early farmers in the region dug up its abundant limestone to use as fence posts. They would have used wood for their fences, but limestone was more plentiful than trees on the prairie. Limestone fence posts can still be seen along many roads in the area.

The Red Hills area in southern Kansas is dry and has few trees. The area got its name from the color of the soil, which is red because it contains iron oxide, or rust. The Red Hills are flat on top, just like the mesas and buttes in the deserts of Arizona and New Mexico.

## Lakes and Rivers

The state's largest river, the Missouri, actually forms Kansas's northeastern border and is the only Kansas waterway large enough for barges. Within the borders of the state, there are two main river systems. The Kansas, or Kaw, River system drains smaller rivers and streams in the northern part of the state. The Arkansas River system drains much of southern Kansas. Throughout the 1800s, the Arkansas River often flooded. Since farmers began

**Average January temperature**
Wichita: 30°F (-1°C)
Topeka: 27°F (-3°C)

**Average July temperature**
Wichita: 80°F (27°C)
Topeka: 79°F (26°C)

**Average yearly rainfall**
Wichita:
 32 inches (81 cm)
Topeka:
 32 inches (81 cm)

**Average yearly snowfall**
Wichita:
 16 inches (41 cm)
Topeka:
 21 inches (53 cm)

### Major Rivers

**Missouri River**
2,315 miles (3,725 km)

**Arkansas River**
1,450 miles (2,333 km)

**Kansas (or Kaw) River**
170 miles (273 km)

### Largest Lakes

**Tuttle Creek Lake**
53,600 acres
 (21,692 ha)

**Milford Lake**
33,000 acres
 (13,355 ha)

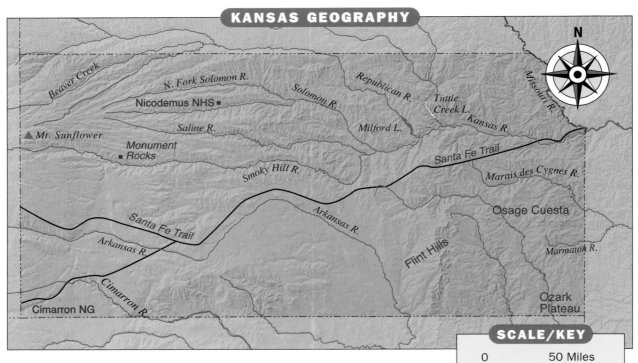

Map labels: Beaver Creek, N. Fork Solomon R., Nicodemus NHS ■, Solomon R., Republican R., Tuttle Creek L., Missouri R., Mt. Sunflower ▲, Saline R., Milford L., Kansas R., Santa Fe Trail, Monument Rocks ■, Smoky Hill R., Marais des Cygnes R., Santa Fe Trail, Arkansas R., Osage Cuesta, Arkansas R., Flint Hills, Marmaton R., Cimarron R., Ozark Plateau, Cimarron NG

**SCALE/KEY**

| 0 | 50 Miles |
| 0 | 50 Kilometers |

*NHS* National Historic Site

*NG* National Grasslands

▲ Highest Point

Mountains

diverting its waters for irrigation, however, the river sometimes nearly dries up. Rainfall in the region is too infrequent to replace the water that is used for irrigation. In fact, in some years the river can become almost completely dry in parts of western Kansas.

Most of the approximately 150 lakes in Kansas are artificially created, including the state's largest lake, Tuttle Creek. Among the other large, artificially created lakes in Kansas are Milford, Cedar Bluff, Kanopolis, and Lovewell. Many of these lakes are drinking-water reservoirs.

## Kansas Climate

Because Kansas lies on the Great Plains, freezing winds from Canada sweep south in the winter and blistering hot winds sweep north in the summer. Kansas is also a prime area for dangerous tornadoes. Kansas is ranked third in the number of tornadoes that strike the United States each year. In fact, Kansas, along with neighbors Texas and Oklahoma, is part of an area in the United States described as "Tornado Alley" by weather experts. Every Kansan learns at an early age how to prepare for these dark funnels that form over the plains. Underground shelters have been built across the state to protect people from tornadoes.

Precipitation falls more in some parts of Kansas than in others, and drought has been a serious problem, most

**DID YOU KNOW?**

It is not unusual in some parts of western Kansas for small streams to flow a short distance and then disappear because there is not enough water to feed them.

notably during the 1930s. Even though the average annual rainfall varies from less than 20 inches (51 cm) in one part of the state to more than 40 inches (102 cm) in another part, floods are a danger because the land around most river basins is relatively flat and low.

## Plants and Wildlife

Kansas is home to about eighty species of mammals, mainly smaller animals such as raccoons, muskrats, and squirrels. There are over four hundred types of birds, including the state bird, the western meadowlark; game birds such as pheasants; and several species of hawks. Kansas has more than sixty species of reptiles, including two kinds of poisonous snakes — copperheads and rattlesnakes — as well as twenty thousand kinds of invertebrates. Endangered animals in Kansas include the sturgeon, the graybelly salamander, the bald eagle, the peregrine falcon, the whooping crane, and the black-footed ferret.

Kansas is also the setting for some of the most beautiful wildflower areas in the country. Asters, columbines, and sunflowers grow in many regions. The state tree, the cottonwood, grows mainly in river basins and is notable for the cottony "snow" given off by its blossoms in the spring.

### Twister Terms

**anvil:** a flat cloud formation at the top of a raging thunderstorm. Tornadoes often follow.

**anvil zits:** lightning flashes in an anvil.

**barber pole:** clouds below an anvil that appear curved or twisted — an early tornado warning sign.

**rope:** a narrow cloud funnel that occurs at the end of a tornado.

**wedge:** a very large tornado that is as wide as it is tall.

**F scale:** a ranking of the strength of a tornado. F1 is the weakest; F5 is the strongest.

▼ Meandering creeks like this one wind through the Kansas flatlands.

# Making a Living in Kansas

> It cost something to develop this fine country of ours, but he that looketh upon it now with all the advantages of wealth, luxury, education, and sense will agree with me when I say that it was worth the price.
>
> — *Robert Stone, Speaker of the Kansas State House of Representatives,* Reminiscences of the Past, *1923*

Kansas is one of the top wheat producing (and milling) states in the nation. Beef cattle and related industries such as meat processing and packing are also important to the state's economy. More than 47 million acres (19 million ha), or about 90 percent of the land, is farmed.

While Kansas leads the nation in many areas of agricultural production, two-thirds of all Kansans live in towns and cities. Two of the main industries in these urban areas are aircraft and automobile manufacturing. Since Americans first took to the skies in "flying machines," the aircraft industry has been one of the state's key industries. Kansas is the world leader in the manufacturing of general aviation aircraft.

## The Nation's Breadbasket

One of the world's largest single agricultural crops has developed from the Turkey Red winter wheat the Mennonites brought with them in the 1870s, as well as from other wheat strains. Kansas harvests about one-fifth of all U.S. wheat. Not surprisingly, Kansas possesses the nation's largest capacity for grain storage, with two of the world's largest grain elevators in Hutchinson and Kansas City.

◀ Kansas's Turkey Red winter wheat.

| Top Employers (of workers age sixteen and over) | |
| --- | --- |
| Services | 26.1% |
| Wholesale and retail trade | 20.8% |
| Manufacturing | 16.8% |
| Transportation, communications, and public utilities | 7.5% |
| Finance, insurance, and real estate | 6.3% |
| Construction | 5.3% |
| Agriculture, forestry, and fisheries | 5.2% |
| Public Administration | 4.4% |
| Mining | 1.0% |

## KANSAS ECONOMY

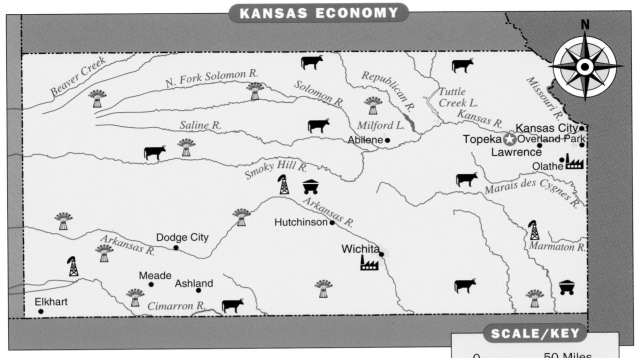

Two other crops, corn and sorghum, rank next in total production. Kansas is the nation's largest producer of sorghum, which is mostly used to feed livestock. Sugar beets, alfalfa, onions, and honeydew melons are other crops that are important to the state's economy.

Kansas, unlike many states today, does not depend on Texas for its beef cattle — it has its own livestock industry. Each year, one of the nation's largest cattle roundups takes place in Elkhart. Altogether, the gross state product of Kansas farms is worth almost $2 billion each year.

### SCALE/KEY

| | |
|---|---|
| 0 — 50 Miles | |
| 0 — 50 Kilometers | |

🌾 Agriculture
🐄 Livestock
🏭 Manufacturing
🛒 Mining
⛽ Oil
⬜ Urban Areas

## Kansas Gross State Product — Millions of dollars

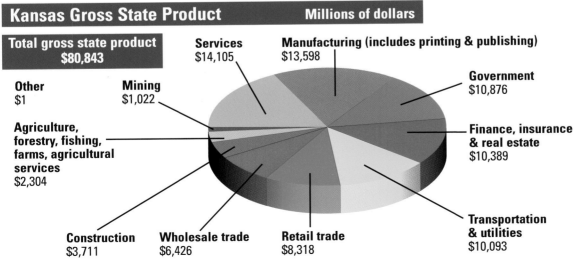

**Total gross state product $80,843**

Services $14,105

Manufacturing (includes printing & publishing) $13,598

Government $10,876

Other $1

Mining $1,022

Agriculture, forestry, fishing, farms, agricultural services $2,304

Finance, insurance & real estate $10,389

Transportation & utilities $10,093

Construction $3,711

Wholesale trade $6,426

Retail trade $8,318

## Industry

In the last half of the twentieth century, more than eighteen hundred new industries moved into the state. Today, "America's Breadbasket" has almost as many manufacturing plants as it has farms. Kansas now ranks first in the nation in flour production.

The most significant manufacturing business is the aircraft industry. Wichita leads the world in production of personal airplanes, with factories of such industry giants as Cessna, Bombardier/Learjet, and Raytheon (formerly Beech). More private aircraft are built in Wichita than in all the rest of the United States combined.

The aircraft industry in Kansas began in 1920 when Jake Moellendick, a successful oil driller, decided to invest his earnings in the development of the first commercially produced airplane, called the Laird Swallow. Clyde Cessna and Walter Beech were other Kansas pioneers in airplane manufacturing. By the mid-1920s, Wichita was known as the air capital of the world. At least fifteen different manufacturers were turning out aircraft or aircraft components there. Only four, however, survived the stock market crash of 1929. In 1999, three Kansas aviation companies made more than two out of every three private planes sold in the world. These companies employ more than forty-three thousand workers in Wichita.

## Mineral Production

Kansas was the first state west of the Mississippi River to have a commercial oil well. The first wells were drilled in the western area of the state in 1892. Since then, the state

### Made in Kansas

**Leading farm products and crops**
Cattle
Wheat
Corn
Sorghum
Soybeans

**Other products**
Transportation equipment
Processed food
Printed goods

▼ A classic 1950 Cessna airplane.

| Major Airports | | |
| --- | --- | --- |
| Airport | Location | Passengers per year (2000) |
| Mid-Continent Airport | Wichita | 1,227,083 |
| Manhattan Regional Airport | Manhattan | 31,500 |
| Salina Municipal Airport | Salina | 6,407 |

has grown to become a major U.S. oil producer. A natural extension of the oil business is natural gas.

Oil drilling also led to the discovery of huge salt deposits in Kansas. Today, Hutchinson is one of the nation's leading salt processing and mining centers. More than twenty different minerals are mined and processed commercially in Kansas, among them quartzite, lead, and zinc.

## Transportation

Modern transportation reached Kansas as early as 1819 when a steamboat steamed up the Missouri River. The state's interior rivers, however, were not deep enough for commercial traffic, so overland routes evolved. The Santa Fe, Oregon, and Chisholm Trails were used for transportation and travel for many years. In the 1850s, mail stagecoaches of the Leavenworth and Pikes Peak Express Company departed daily for the seventeen-day round trip to Denver. The first interstate railroad to reach Kansas arrived at its borders in 1860. By 1868, the railroads were building westward from Topeka, and the Kansas Pacific line reached Denver in 1870. Like most U.S. citizens, Kansans now use cars as their main form of transportation.

## The Service Industry

More Kansans work in service industry jobs than in any other industry. In this type of work, people help other people or businesses. Service industry employers include restaurants, banks, and hospitals. Other service workers sell the flour, beef, airplanes, and railway cars manufactured in the state. Combined service industry jobs account for one-third of all employment in Kansas.

▼ A salt mine in Hutchinson.

KANSAS 27

# Governing the Sunflower State

The Governor's salary was $2,000 per annum. He was allowed $240 for rent, $100 for furniture for his office, $100 for stationery, $75 for postage, $40 for fuel and lights, $1,000 for secret service, and $600 for a private secretary.

*— William E. Connelley, historian, describing the salary and expenses of the first state governor, from A History of Kansas and Kansans, 1918*

On January 29, 1861, after one of the bloodiest periods ever experienced by any territory, Kansas entered the Union as the thirty-fourth state. Kansan lawmakers and citizens had hoped to enter the Union a year earlier, but Article 6 in the Kansas Bill of Rights kept it out. This article stated that slavery was not allowed in Kansas. Before the Civil War, pro-slavery lawmakers in Congress refused to admit a state that prohibited slavery into the Union. Since Southern lawmakers, who were overwhelmingly pro-slavery, controlled Congress in 1860, Kansans had to wait for the election of 1860 and hope that Republicans gained control of Congress. They did. President James Buchanan signed the bill admitting Kansas to the Union. The Civil War broke out three months later.

In creating a state constitution, Kansas lawmakers followed the model of the U.S. Constitution that set up laws and branches of government. The Kansas Constitution, like the U.S. Constitution, divides the government into three branches: executive, legislative, and judicial.

## The Executive Branch

Kansas elects a governor and five other officials every four years. The elected governor then chooses twelve people to head state agencies such as the Department of Agriculture and the Department of Wildlife and Parks. The state senate must approve these officials, who are known as members of the governor's cabinet.

### Landons of Kansas

In 1979, Nancy Landon Kassebaum of Topeka became the first woman who was not the widow of a U.S. congressman to be elected to the Senate. A Republican, she served in the Senate until 1997. Her father, Alfred Landon, was governor of Kansas from 1933 to 1937. In 1936 he ran for president against Franklin Roosevelt and won only two states, neither of them Kansas.

| Elected Posts in the Executive Branch | | |
|---|---|---|
| Office | Length of Term | Term Limits |
| Governor | 4 years | 2 consecutive terms |
| Lieutenant governor | 4 years | 2 consecutive terms |
| Secretary of State | 4 years | 2 consecutive terms |
| Attorney General | 4 years | 2 consecutive terms |
| Treasurer | 4 years | 2 consecutive terms |
| State Insurance Commissioner | 4 years | none |

The governor and the lieutenant governor can serve only two four-year terms in a row, but they can be elected to an unlimited number of terms. The lieutenant governor serves in the governor's place if the governor is unable to complete a term.

## The Legislative Branch

The Kansas legislative branch of government is divided into a senate and a house of representatives. There are 125 members in the house of representatives, each of whom is elected for two years. The state has forty senators elected to four-year terms. There are no term limits in the legislative branch. The legislature meets every year. In even-numbered years, the meeting of the legislature is not allowed to last more than ninety days unless two-thirds of the members agree to extra sessions. The legislature's main responsibilities include funding the state government, passing laws, and holding sessions for the people of Kansas to discuss important issues.

## The Judicial Branch

The Kansas Supreme Court is the highest court in the state. Kansas Supreme Court judges are appointed by the governor. After the first year in office, Kansans get to vote on whether to retain each justice. If the retention vote is in the justice's favor, he or she serves a six-year term. Most cases that come before the supreme court are appeals, or reviews, of decisions made by

either the state court of appeals or one of the district courts. A person involved in a court case may seek an appeal when the person believes that the first court's decision was wrong. The court of appeals, which has ten judges, is the court below the supreme court. Sometimes all ten judges hear a case together, but they usually divide into panels of three. This court is located in Topeka, but judges often travel to other places in the state to hear cases.

Kansas is divided into six judicial departments and, within these departments, thirty-one judicial districts. Each district has a court that handles all civil and criminal cases, including divorces and juvenile matters. Each county has one district court and at least one judge who lives in and serves the county. Some counties also have judicial magistrates, who, unlike judges, do not have to be lawyers.

Municipal courts deal with legal issues within cities. If someone breaks a municipal (city) law or has a case against a city, his or her case is heard first in municipal court. Decisions made in the municipal court can be appealed to the district courts; district court decisions can be appealed to the court of appeals; and decisions in this court may be appealed to the supreme court.

## Local Government

Because Kansas is a large state with widely separated communities, a great deal of local political action takes place at the county, rather than city or town, level. In fact, county government is the main form of government at the local level, providing services such as road maintenance, education, child welfare, consumer protection, job training, and water quality. Kansas's 105 counties have elected officials with positions ranging from sheriffs to board of education members to attorneys,

▼ The current Kansas governor's mansion in Topeka was built in 1928 and became the official residence in 1962. (Before that, Kansas governors lived in Bennett House, a much older structure.) The house is set on 200 acres (81 ha) of land, and its nature, walking, and jogging trails are open to the public.

## The White House via Kansas

### DWIGHT DAVID EISENHOWER (1953–1961)

Born in Dennison, Texas, Dwight David Eisenhower (1890–1969) was one of the most admired men and popular presidents ever to serve the nation. Eisenhower was born the third of seven sons. The family settled in Abilene, Kansas, in 1891. Eisenhower graduated from Abilene High School in 1909 and worked in a local creamery for two years before entering the U.S. Military Academy at West Point.

In 1915, Eisenhower graduated from West Point and was commissioned as a second lieutenant. His graduating class produced an astonishing fifty-nine generals in later years. Eisenhower married Mamie Doud in 1916. Over the next twenty years, he rose to the top ranks of the military.

In 1942, less than a year after the United States entered World War II, Eisenhower became a household name when he was named Commander-in-Chief of Allied Forces in Africa. In 1943, he became Supreme Commander of the Allied Expeditionary Forces and commanded the D-Day invasion of Normandy on June 6, 1944.

After the war, Eisenhower became the first commander of the North Atlantic Treaty Organization (NATO). He retired from the army in 1948 to serve as president of Columbia University in New York City and in 1952 resigned his commission to announce his candidacy for the Republican Party nomination for president. Campaign buttons at the time carried the slogan "I Like Ike," referring to Eisenhower by his nickname. Elected on November 4, 1952, "Ike" served two terms as president of the United States, from January 20, 1953 to January 20, 1961. During Eisenhower's years in office, the Korean War ended, Alaska and Hawaii became states, and the U.S. Supreme Court issued the landmark decision in *Brown v. Board of Education*. Eisenhower used federal troops to enforce integration and was the major force behind the interstate highway system that was built during the 1950s. After leaving office, Eisenhower lived and worked in Gettysburg, Pennsylvania. He is buried at the Eisenhower Presidential Center in Abilene.

tax collectors, and clerks. A board of commissioners consisting of between three and five members, depending on the population of the county, is the administrative branch of county government. Commissioners serve four-year terms, and there are no term limits.

| State Legislature | | | |
|---|---|---|---|
| House | Number of Members | Length of Term | Term Limits |
| Senate | 40 senators | 4 years | none |
| House of Representatives | 125 representatives | 2 years | none |

# Get a Kick from Kansas

Oh, they told me out in Kansas
Oh, they told me out in Kansas,
Yes, they told me there I'd find
That the money grew like apples on the trees.

— *George Vinton Graham, American folk singer, 1938*

Kansans have always been hardworking. Life on the frontier, on farms, and in growing cities left little time for leisure. Life in the Sunflower State, however, is not all work and no play. Today, visitors can discover lots of fun things to do and see, both indoors and out.

The best place to start a tour of Kansas is probably the state capital, Topeka. Perhaps the most interesting building to visit is the state capitol itself. Many Kansans consider it the most beautiful building in the state. It is located on 20 acres (8 ha) of land in downtown Topeka. On the grounds leading to the building are bronze statues of Abraham Lincoln, a pioneer mother and child, and a 9-foot (3-m) statue of Astra, a Kaw warrior. There is also a star-shaped Law Enforcement Memorial with the names of Kansas police officers who died in the line of duty as well as a Statue of Liberty replica donated by the Boy Scouts of America. On permanent display are limestone statues of some of the state's greatest sons and daughters, including aviator Amelia Earhart and William Allen White, a famous journalist. At a height of 304 feet (93 m), the five-story Kansas Capitol Dome is higher than the United States Capitol Dome in Washington, D.C.

The state capitol isn't the only place to see in Topeka. The Kansas Museum of History contains exhibits on Kansas life

▼ Kansas sculptor Robert Merrell Gage created the sculpture *Pioneer Mother and Child* in an homage to early settlers.

DEDICATED TO THE PIONEER WOMEN OF KANSAS

from prehistoric through modern times. There are exhibits on a variety of topics including the early peoples of the region, the Santa Fe and Oregon Trails, farming, and transportation. Objects in the museum's collection include a recreation of a Wichita grass lodge, a Victorian dollhouse, and a 1914 biplane. A stop at the world-famous Topeka Zoological Park should be part of a visit as well. Black Bear Woods is a 20,000-square foot (1,858-sq m) habitat where two black bears and two red foxes live together much as they would in the wild. This zoo was the first to build a glass tunnel under its gorilla exhibit for visitors to watch these huge animals up close.

For aviation fans, there is the Combat Air Museum. This small museum in the southern part of Topeka is home to more than twenty aircraft used in U.S. combat.

## Moving West

West of Topeka is the city of Abilene, the location of the Dwight D. Eisenhower Presidential Center. Built at the childhood home of the thirty-fourth president, the center contains exhibits of Eisenhower's lifetime accomplishments.

▲ Topeka's Combat Air Museum features warplanes from World War I to the jet age.

**DID YOU KNOW?**

**H**ays House, a restaurant in Council Grove, has been open since 1857, making it the oldest continuously-operating restaurant west of the Mississippi.

Travelers often leave the main highway about 20 miles (32 km) west of Topeka to follow the Skyline-Millcreek Scenic Drive. This country road winds through the rolling area known as the Flint Hills. It is beautiful any time of year, but especially when the flowers bloom in spring and when the prairie grass becomes flaming red in autumn. As it moves west, the road leads to Rolling Hills Refuge. Among the surprising sights here are tigers and camels. This 145-acre (58-ha) refuge is home to more than eighty animal species from around the world, many of them endangered. Visitors may see anything from Nile River lizards to an Indian rhinoceros to North American mountain lions.

▲ **A lion at Rolling Hills Refuge.**

## Heading South

Heading south from Abilene brings travelers to Wichita, the largest city in Kansas and home to Exploration Place. Opened in 2000, this children's museum, science center, and outdoor recreation area offers something for everyone. Among its many features are three interactive theaters, a miniature golf course, a huge electric train set, and flight simulators. There are a number of other museums to see in Wichita. The Kansas African-American Museum has many exhibits on an integral part of the state's history. The Kansas Aviation Museum provides an overview of the history of flight, including Kansas's contributions to that history.

## The Plains

Moving west across the plains of southern Kansas brings sightseers to the small town of Greensburg. Underneath the green water tower at the town's center is the world's largest hand-dug well. The hole was dug straight down into the ground for more than 100 feet (31 m) — a depth equal to more than twenty kids standing on one another's shoulders. In 1888, town leaders paid from fifty cents to one dollar a day to each worker. The hole grew to be 32 feet (10 m) across and 109 feet (33 m) deep before striking water. The workers

### Forever and Ever

The town of Lindsborg, which was settled by Swedish immigrants in the nineteenth century, has a tradition that is more than one hundred years old. Every year since 1889, local Bethany College has presented a performance of Handel's *Messiah,* one of the best-loved pieces of music in the Western classical tradition. The annual performance, which takes place during Easter week, has grown into a festival that includes performances of works by many other classical composers. The *Messiah* chorus includes 550 singers and a 65-piece accompanying orchestra.

even lowered a mule into the well to help with construction of the well's bottom. Today visitors only need to walk down a stairway into this hole to see the water's surface.

In the prairie town of Meade, just a little farther west, visitors can see the hideout of the famous Dalton Gang. In the days of the Wild West, this gang of brothers robbed banks and stagecoaches and killed several innocent people. The Daltons seemed to disappear every time they rode off to the town of Meade. That is because the gang hid in an underground tunnel beneath the house of their sister, Eva Whipple.

Miles of expansive prairie lie north of Meade. Outside of Scott City, in west-central Kansas, are towering arches of white rocks spread across the land. These are the famous Monument Rocks formations carved into chalk that once lay at the bottom of prehistoric seas. They rise as tall as 60 feet (18 m). Pioneers in the 1800s used the rocks as a landmark when traveling across the wide, empty prairies.

Anyone fascinated with cow towns and gunslingers will want to stop by Dodge City — the Cowboy Capital of the World. This colorful town offers visitors the chance to imagine what life was like during the time of Bat Masterson and the Wild West. Front Street, Dodge City's main road in the 1870s, has been recreated at the Boot Hill Museum, where visitors can participate in many activities.

In the northeastern part of the state, Lawrence is home to the University of Kansas. The amazing Kansas Natural

▼ A replica of Front Street in Dodge City offers a glimpse into Western life in the late 1800s.

History Museum is also in Lawrence. In the museum are the fossil skeletons of many creatures that lived in Kansas long before people did, including a rhinoceros from prehistoric times. A realistic diorama shows scenes of life in Kansas during the times before white explorers arrived.

## Communications

It has been said that Kansas is perhaps the only place where a newspaper started before there was any news to print. It has also been said that the history of journalism in Kansas is unique. The first newspaper published in the state, the *Shawnee Sun* (1835), was printed entirely in the Native American Shawnee language.

The first regular weekly paper was the *Kansas Weekly Herald of Leavenworth* (1854). Over the years, Kansas has had a record of more newspapers per capita than any other state. In an eighty-year period, between 1854 and 1936, over 4,386 newspapers were published. The papers served to keep everyone across the state connected.

## Special Events and Places

Rodeos and roundups help keep the traditions of the Wild West alive in Kansas. Throughout the state, crowds cheer as cowboys rope calves, ride bulls and bucking broncos, and

▼ A rodeo rider wrestles a steer. Steer roping is one of the oldest events in professional rodeo.

wrestle steers to the ground. Rodeos are held almost every weekend during the summer months.

## Sports

While Kansas has no major league professional teams, it is home to a United States Hockey League (USHL) team, the Topeka Scarecrows. It is basketball, however, that has the tightest grip on the state's heart.

Since basketball was first invented in 1891, Kansans have been fans. The University of Kansas Jayhawks basketball team consistently draws sellout crowds to its games. Some of the greatest players and coaches in basketball history grew up, coached, or played basketball in Kansas.

Wilt Chamberlain was one of basketball's all-time great men. "Wilt the Stilt" stood 7 feet 1 inch (2.2 m) tall. He was an All-American for the University of Kansas in 1957 and 1958 and went on to become the second-leading scorer in the history of professional basketball.

Adolph Rupp, from Halstead, played on two college championship teams at Kansas University in 1922 and 1923. Rupp, later known as the Baron of Basketball, coached at the University of Kentucky for forty-two seasons and became the winningest coach in college basketball until his record was broken in 1997.

Billie Jean Moore, one of the most successful coaches in the history of women's basketball, was born in Westmoreland and raised in Topeka. Moore coached the first U.S. Women's Olympic basketball team in 1976 when the team won the silver medal. Fellow Kansan Lynette Woodard is a four-time All-American player from the University of Kansas and a gold medal-winning member of the 1984 U.S. Olympic women's team. Woodard is the all-time leading scorer in women's college basketball. Raised in Wichita, Woodard became the first female player on the Harlem Globetrotters, a world-famous men's team.

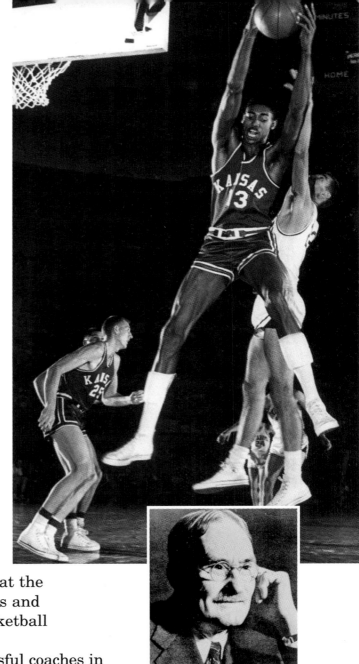

▲ Wilt Chamberlain (*top*) leaps for a rebound in a 1957 college game. Canadian James Naismith (*inset*), "the father of basketball," was the basketball coach for thirty-nine years at the University of Kansas.

# Famous Kansans

*Toto, I've a feeling we're not in Kansas anymore.*
— *Dorothy, in the movie* The Wizard of Oz, *1939*
*(Line written by screenwriters Noel Langley,*
*Florence Ryerson, and Edgar Allen Wolfe.)*

**Following are only a few of the thousands of people who were born, died, or spent much of their lives in Kansas and made extraordinary contributions to the state and the nation.**

## CARRY A. NATION
### TEMPERANCE CRUSADER
**BORN:** *November 28, 1846, Garrard County, KY*
**DIED:** *June 9, 1911, Abilene*

**B**orn Carry Amelia Monroe, Carry Nation was perhaps the best-known leader of the temperance movement against alcohol in the late nineteenth century. Her hatred of alcohol began as a young woman when, in 1867, she left her first husband, an alcoholic, who died shortly thereafter. In 1877, she married David Nation. Although Kansas had passed the first prohibition laws in 1880, saloons continued to operate in the state. Nation argued that since they were illegal, there would be nothing wrong in her physically destroying any saloon she could find. In the 1890s, she moved to Kansas and led several hatchet-swinging, saloon-smashing attacks there and in large cities throughout the country. She was arrested more than thirty times before her retirement due to poor health.

## NAT LOVE
### COWBOY
**BORN:** *June, 1854, Davidson County, TN*
**DIED:** *circa 1921, Los Angeles, CA*

**N**at Love was born into slavery in Tennessee in 1854. As a boy, Love learned the skills of roping, herding, and branding cattle and horses. After the Civil War, he moved to Kansas to find work as a cowboy. He was soon driving cattle up the trails from

Texas to Kansas. Love earned the nickname "Deadwood Dick" for his stellar performance at a rodeo in Deadwood. He was a working cowboy for most of his life. When he retired, Love became a Pullman porter on the transcontinental railroad. He once said that it was "still exciting to ride across the great mountains and wide plains, even if one had to do it for tips."

# WALTER JOHNSON
## BASEBALL PLAYER

**BORN:** *November 6, 1887, Humboldt*
**DIED:** *December 10, 1946, Washington, D.C.*

**J**ohnson spent his twenty-one-season major league career with the Washington Senators, winning 417 games — the second most in major league history. He pitched 110 shutouts, a major league record. One of the hardest-throwing players in baseball history, Johnson led the American League in strikeouts twelve times. Known by fans and players as "The Big Train," Johnson was elected to baseball's Hall of Fame in 1936.

JOHNSON, WASHINGTON

# BUSTER KEATON
## ACTOR

**BORN:** *October 4, 1895, Piqua*
**DIED:** *February 1, 1966, Woodland Hills, CA*

**J**oseph Frank "Buster" Keaton was one of the greatest stars of the early silent film industry. Known as "The Great Stone Face" for his expressionless face, he was also highly praised for his physical comedy antics. After appearing with his parents in a vaudeville act, Keaton went to Hollywood and made fourteen films between 1917 and 1920. Between 1920 and 1923, Keaton wrote, directed, and acted in twenty short films. Of these, *The General* and *Steamboat Bill* are considered among the greatest films ever produced. His fame declined in the 1930s, but he continued to appear in movies until his death in 1966.

# AMELIA EARHART
## AVIATOR

**BORN:** *July 24, 1897, Atchison*
**DIED:** *Disappeared July 2, 1937, near Howland Island, Pacific Ocean*

**A**melia Earhart was one of the great aviators of the early twentieth century. In 1928, she became the first woman to fly across the Atlantic Ocean as a passenger. Earhart subsequently made a solo flight across the Atlantic in 1932, and in the process she set a speed record of fourteen hours and fifty-six minutes. Three years later, Earhart became the first person to fly alone from Honolulu to California. In recognition of her achievement, she was awarded the Distinguished Flying Cross, the first woman to be so honored. In 1937, she attempted to fly around the world at the equator. She and her navigator Frederick Noonan completed the first 22,000 miles (35,398 km) of the trip on schedule. Then, on July 2, 1937, the pair took off from New Guinea. After six hours, contact was lost and the two were never heard from again. Extensive searches for Earhart revealed no wreckage, and her true fate has never been determined.

## JOHN STEUART CURRY
**PAINTER**

**BORN:** *November 14, 1897, Jefferson County*
**DIED:** *August 29, 1946, Madison, WI*

Curry was a famous painter whose murals about the life of abolitionist and Free Soiler John Brown can be seen in the state capitol building in Topeka. Curry first gained attention for drawings he did for the Ringling Brothers Circus in 1932. He is known for paintings that are uniquely American. Other works by Curry include *Tornado Over Kansas* (1929) and *The Mississippi* (1935).

## EMMETT KELLY
**CLOWN**

**BORN:** *December 9, 1898, Sedan*
**DIED:** *March 28, 1979, Sarasota, FL*

Kelly was one of the most beloved clowns in circus history. He worked at an advertising agency before his clowning career took off. Kelly was more than forty years old when his sad-faced hobo, "Weary Willie," became a character in the Ringling Brothers circus. People all over the world saw a photo of Kelly, wearing his clown pants, carrying water to try to put out the tragic Hartford Circus Fire in 1944. He also appeared on stage, on television, and in film.

## STAN KENTON
**MUSICIAN**

**BORN:** *February 19, 1912, Wichita*
**DIED:** *August 25, 1979, Hollywood, CA*

Born in Kansas, Stanley Kenton moved with his family to Los Angeles as a child. His mother, a piano teacher, was the first to recognize his talents as a pianist. As soon as he graduated from high school, Stan began playing with local jazz bands in bars and clubs. He was thirty when he formed his first band in 1941. Kenton's music was experimental, incorporating elements of both classical music and Afro-Cuban rhythms. This music, which was known as progressive jazz or cool jazz, drew large audiences of young fans. Kenton once said, "Some of the wise boys who say my music is loud, blatant and that's all should see the faces of the kids who have driven a hundred miles through the snow to see the band . . . to stand in front of the bandstand in an ecstasy all their own." In later years, Kenton opened a music school, started a record label, and continued to tour the country with his band.

## GORDON PARKS
**PHOTOGRAPHER**

**BORN:** *November 30, 1912, Fort Scott*

Gordon Parks left home at the age of sixteen. While working as a waiter on trains of the Northern Pacific Line, he was inspired by magazine pictures to become a photographer. Parks trained himself and, with the help of Marva Louis, the wife of famous boxer Joe Louis, became a well-known fashion photographer in Chicago. In 1941, he won a scholarship and the opportunity to work for the Farm Security Administration (FSA) in Washington. As an FSA photographer, Parks documented the lives of African Americans in the nation's capital, exposing inequality and racism at the center of U.S. life. From 1948 to 1972, Parks was a photographer for *Life* magazine. He has published many books, including *The Learning Tree* and *Half Past Autumn*. The multi-talented Parks has also directed movies and composed musical scores.

# WILLIAM INGE
**PLAYWRIGHT**

BORN: *May 3, 1913, Independence*
DIED: *June 10, 1973, New York, NY*

**W**illiam Inge first became interested in the theater when his Boy Scout troop was invited to attend performances in his hometown of Independence. After college he became a professor and theater critic. Working as a theater critic inspired him to write plays. Inge wrote about life in small towns, once saying, "I've always been glad I grew up in Independence, because I feel it gave me a knowledge of people and a love of people." In 1953, Inge won the Pulitzer Prize for his play *Picnic*, which was based on the lives of women he had known as a child. Film versions of Inge's plays, *Come Back, Little Sheba* (1953), with Burt Lancaster; *Picnic* (1954), with William Holden and Kim Novak; and *Bus Stop* (1956), starring Marilyn Monroe, were major successes.

# BOB DOLE
**STATESMAN**

BORN: *July 22, 1923, Russell*

**S**enate majority leader, chairman of the Republican Party, vice-presidential and presidential candidate, Robert Dole was in the spotlight of U.S. politics for the latter third of the twentieth century. During World War II Dole served as an officer in the U.S. Army's 10th Mountain Division. In 1945, while fighting in Italy, Dole was hit by machine gun fire. Dole survived his wounds with a shattered right shoulder and nonfunctional arm. He was twice decorated for heroic achievement, receiving two Purple Hearts and the Bronze Star Medal. After a successful career as a lawyer and state politician, Dole ran for the U.S. Senate in 1968 and won. In 1971, he became chairman of the Republican National Committee. In 1976, President Gerald Ford chose Dole as his vice-presidential running mate. Ford and Dole lost the election, but Dole continued to serve as senator. In 1984, he was elected Senate Majority Leader and set a record as the longest-serving Republican leader, holding the position until 1996 when he resigned from the Senate to campaign for president. Dole lost the election to the incumbent, President Bill Clinton. Bob Dole is married to Elizabeth Hanford Dole, also a leader in the Republican Party. Among other high-profile posts, she served as Secretary of Transportation under President Ronald Reagan.

# Kansas
## History At-A-Glance

**1541**
Francisco Vásquez de Coronado reaches present-day Kansas.

**1803**
Present-day Kansas, part of the Louisiana Territory, is purchased by the United States.

**1835**
First newspaper in Kansas, the *Shawnee Sun,* is printed in the native Shawnee language.

**1854**
Kansas is organized as a territory. The Kansas-Nebraska Act is passed and signed by President Franklin Pierce.

**1856–58**
Violence in "Bleeding Kansas" breaks out in several areas of the territory between pro-slavery and antislavery forces.

**1861**
Kansas becomes the 34th state, with Topeka as its capital.

**1869–73**
Five railroad companies lay track across Kansas.

**1880**
An amendment to the Kansas Constitution prohibits manufacture, sale, or gifts of all forms of alcohol.

**1882**
Dodge City is the "cowboy capital" of the West during the days of the great cattle empires.

**1887**
The first woman mayor in the country, Susan Madora Salter, is elected in Argonia.

**1903**
The Kansas State Capitol building in Topeka is completed.

**1912**
Women in Kansas win the right to vote in all state elections.

---

**1600**      **1700**      **1800**

---

**1492**
Christopher Columbus comes to New World.

**1607**
Capt. John Smith and three ships land on Virginia coast and start first English settlement in New World — Jamestown.

**1754–63**
French and Indian War.

**1773**
Boston Tea Party.

**1776**
Declaration of Independence adopted July 4.

**1777**
Articles of Confederation adopted by Continental Congress.

**1787**
U.S. Constitution written.

**1812–14**
War of 1812.

# United States
## History At-A-Glance

**1920**
The Laird Swallow, the first manufactured plane in the country, is built in Wichita.

**1930s**
Drought makes the state part of the "Dust Bowl."

**1937**
Amelia Earhart disappears over the Pacific Ocean during an attempt to become the first woman to pilot a plane around the world.

**1953**
Dwight D. Eisenhower, of Abilene, is sworn in as the 34th president of the United States.

**1954**
The U.S. Supreme Court rules in *Brown v. The Board of Education of Topeka, Kansas* that racially segregated schools are unconstitutional.

**1956**
The Kansas Turnpike is completed.

**1978**
Nancy Landon Kassebaum is elected the first woman U.S. Senator, from Kansas.

**1984**
Lynette Woodard is named captain of the U.S. women's basketball team that wins the Olympic gold medal.

**1988**
University of Kansas Jayhawks win the national collegiate basketball championship.

**1991**
An F5 tornado touches down on the ground for about fifty minutes in south–central Kansas.

**1996**
Bob Dole retires as longest-serving majority leader in the U.S. Senate and is defeated in the presidential race against Bill Clinton.

**2000**
The last full-blooded member of the Kaw Nation dies.

---

**1800**      **1900**      **2000**

---

**1848**
Gold discovered in California draws eighty thousand prospectors in the 1849 Gold Rush.

**1861–65**
Civil War.

**1869**
Transcontinental railroad completed.

**1917–18**
U.S. involvement in World War I.

**1929**
Stock market crash ushers in Great Depression.

**1941–45**
U.S. involvement in World War II.

**1950–53**
U.S. fights in the Korean War.

**1964–73**
U.S. involvement in Vietnam War.

**2000**
George W. Bush wins the closest presidential election in U.S. history.

**2001**
A terrorist attack in which four hijacked airliners crash into New York City's World Trade Center, the Pentagon, and farmland in western Pennsylvania leaves thousands dead or injured.

▼ **An early twentieth-century view of Atchison.**

# Festivals and Fun for All

Check web site for exact date and directions.

### Agriculture Hall of Fame, Bonner Springs

In addition to plaques honoring agricultural innovators such as Squanto, Thomas Jefferson, George Washington Carver, and John Deere, the hall contains relics and works of art. Exhibits feature antique implements, gadgets, and contraptions that were standard equipment in fields and farmhouses of earlier times. A nineteenth-century farm town is also part of the site.
www.aghalloffame.com

### Beef Empire Days Rodeo, Garden City

This rodeo takes place during the first two weeks in June. In addition to the rodeo, events include free barbecue, a square dance, and other entertainment.
www.beefempiredays
rodeo.com

### Big Brutus, West Mineral

Big Brutus is the second-largest power shovel in the world. It stands 160 feet (49 m) tall and weighs 11 million pounds (nearly 5 million kg). From 1963 to 1974, Brutus was used to dig coal from the ground in southeastern Kansas. One scoop of the bucket dug enough coal to fill three railroad cars. Brutus is no longer in use for digging coal. The electric bill to run Brutus simply as a tourist attraction is $27,000 a month.
www.lasr.net/leisure/kansas/crawford/
pittsburg/att1.html

### Civil War on the Border, Olathe

In this annual reenactment, Civil War border skirmishes between Union and Confederate units in Kansas are recreated. The event takes place on the third weekend in April.
www.olathe.org/olathe_cvb/festivalandevents

### Dodge City Days, Dodge City

Every July, this ten-day celebration features more than fifty events, including a rodeo with almost one thousand contestants. Other events include craft shows, children's activities, a Western parade, and a beauty pageant.
www.dodgecitydays.com

### Kansas City Renaissance Festival, Bonner Springs

This event in a town a few miles outside of Kansas City recreates a sixteenth-century European village. People wear period clothing and participate in entertainment of the era.
www.kcrenfest.com

### Kansas City Street Painting Festival, Kansas City

A community, multi-cultural festival draws professional, student, and amateur artists who create chalk "paintings" on sponsored asphalt canvases on the streets of downtown Kansas City.
www.festivals.com/
04-april/streetpainting/
eventlistings.cfm

## Kansas State Fair, Hutchinson

The annual fair showcases Kansas agriculture, industry, and culture. There are more than thirty thousand participants a year.
www.kansasstatefair.com

## The McPherson Scottish Festival and Highland Games, McPherson

This annual cultural event includes a Highland dance competition and a caber toss. Scottish goods are displayed and sold by local craftspeople and chefs.
www.mcpherson.com/418/ community/ scot/festivalinfo.html

## Native American Heritage Museum, Highland

A collection of exhibits about the early peoples native to the Kansas region and those who lived in the region after relocation. Displays focus on the Iowa, Kickapoo, Potawatomi, and Sac and Fox tribes.
www.kshs.org/places/highland.html

◀ A Highland Games participant prepares to toss a caber, a log measuring 22 feet (7m) long and weighing about 125 pounds (57 kg).

## Smoky Hill River Festival, Salina

A weekend summer event comprising music, art, dance, food, races, a kite fest, and other activities. Music performances present country, jazz, blues, pop, oldies, ethnic, and alternative styles.
www.riverfestival.com

## Walnut Valley Bluegrass Festival, Winfield

This festival is a showcase for bluegrass artists from around the state. Artists and craftspeople are also able to sell their work.
www.wvfest.com

## The World's Largest Ball of Twine, Cawker City

What's 40 feet (12 m) around and weighs more than 17,320 pounds (7,856 kg) — as much as three elephants? Twine — a lot of it. In 1953, Frank Stoeber began winding all the string he could get his hands on into a huge ball. Today, that ball contains more than 1,310 miles (2,108 km) of string — enough to reach halfway across the United States!
skyways.lib.ks.us/kansas/towns/Cawker/twine.html

## Books

Deady, Kathleen. *Kansas Facts and Symbols*. Mankato, Minnesota: Bridgestone Books, 2000. Part of a series of books about the states and their symbols, this book includes many interesting facts about Kansas throughout its history.

Harper, Steve. *83,000 Square Miles, Kansas Day Trips*. Wichita: Wichita Eagle and Beacon Publishing, 1998. This travel guide details twenty-seven fun-filled day trips across the state.

Inglish, Howard. *Tornado: Terror and Survival: The Andover Tornado — April 26, 1991*. Andover, Kansas: The Counseling Center of Butler County, 1991. A complete and detailed account of the horrific Andover Tornado that struck in southeast Kansas on April 26, 1991, killing thirteen people and destroying more than 350 homes.

Miller, Nyle, and Joseph Snell. *Great Gunfighters of the Kansas Cowtowns, 1867–1886*. Lincoln: University of Nebraska Press, 1986. A great source for historical accounts of gunfighters and lawmen of the late 1800s, such as Wild Bill Hickock, Wyatt Earp, and many others.

Young, Jeff C. *Dwight D. Eisenhower: Soldier and President*. Greensboro, NC: Morgan Reynolds, 2001. A complete biography covering the major events in, and the interesting details of, Eisenhower's life.

Zeinert, Karen. *Tragic Prelude: Bleeding Kansas*. North Haven, CT: Shoestring Press, 2001. This account of the controversy surrounding the admission of Kansas to the Union makes use of period letters, diaries, and photographs to bring a sense of immediacy to the story.

## Web Sites

▶ Official State Web Site
www.accesskansas.org

▶ State Historical Society Site
www.kshs.org

▶ State Capital Site
www.topeka.org

▶ Prehistoric Kansas
www.oceansofkansas.com

Note: Page numbers in *italics* refer to maps, illustrations, or photographs.